Herbert Howells
Six Pieces for Organ

NOVELLO PUBLISHING LIMITED

Order No: NOV 590354

Contents

No. 1
PRELUDIO 'SINE NOMINE'

H. H. 1940

No. 2
SARABAND
(For the morning of Easter)

allarg. molto

Tempo I

No. 3
MASTER TALLIS'S TESTAMENT

Quasi lento, teneramente ♪ = 60

H.H. 1940

No. 4
FUGUE, CHORALE AND EPILOGUE

Quasi lento, serioso ed espressivo ♩ = 54

tranquillo, teneramente (ma un poco più mosso)

poco a poco un poch. accel.

fff assai sonore

mezza movimento

rall.

fff

p subito e dim.

pesante

subito > *dim. molto*

tranquillo, mesto ma dolce ♪ = 72

May, 1940

No. 5
SARABAND
(In Modo Elegiaco)

Quasi lento, assai espressivo ♩ = 56

cpld. to Sw. *assai sostenuto*

H. H. Sept. 16, 1945

No. 6

PAEAN

Allegro sempre brioso ♩ = 144

più espress., rubato

Vivo assai ♩ = 144

Largamente ♩ = 96

fff Solo Reeds

Solo to Ped.

ff G♮

G♮ to Ped.   *marc.*

allarg. molto

fff

May, 1940

ORGAN ALBUMS

ed Allan Wicks
CANTERBURY ORGAN ALBUM

ed John Sanders
GLOUCESTER ORGAN ALBUM

ed Francis Jackson
YORK ORGAN ALBUM

The first three collections in a unique series featuring music by the organists of England's great cathedrals. Each volume also contains the specification of the cathedral organ together with biographical details and pictures of the composers.

ELGAR ORGAN ALBUM Book 1
Cantique
Adagio from the Cello Concerto
Carillon
Solemn Prelude *In memoriam* from 'For the Fallen'
Imperial March

ELGAR ORGAN ALBUM Book 2
Nimrod from 'Enigma Variations'
Triumphal March from 'Caractacus'
Funeral March from 'Grania and Diarmid'
Prelude and Angel's Farewell from 'The Dream of Gerontius'

PARRY ORGAN ALBUM Book 1
Fantasia and Fugue in G
Chorale Fantasia on 'The Old Hundredth'
Elegy for April 7, 1913

PARRY ORGAN ALBUM Book 2
Toccata and Fugue (The Wanderer)
Chorale Fantasia on 'O God Our Help'
Chorale Fantasia on An Old English Tune

ed Robert Gower
ORGAN MUSIC OF JOHN IRELAND
Sursum Corda
Alla Marcia
Elegiac Romance
Intrada
Villanella
Menuetto
The Holy Boy
Meditation
Capriccio